OF BIRDS AND BONES

For Bird and Chris

best wishes

Geraldine Mitchell

OF BIRDS AND BONES

ARLEN
HOUSE

Of Birds and Bones

is published in 2014 by
ARLEN HOUSE
42 Grange Abbey Road
Baldoyle,
Dublin 13,
Ireland
Phone/Fax: 353–86–8207617
Email: arlenhouse@gmail.com
arlenhouse.blogspot.com

978–1–85132–099–8, paperback

Distributed internationally by
SYRACUSE UNIVERSITY PRESS
621 Skytop Road, Suite 110
Syracuse, NY 13244–5290, USA
Phone: 315–443–5534/Fax: 315–443–5545
Email: supress@syr.edu

Typesetting ¦ Arlen House
Artwork ¦ linocuts by Lisa Molina
'Magpie' (front cover)
'Baobab' (back cover)

CONTENTS

For Lisa and Yann

PROPOSITION

As animals walk barefoot
over earth's thick skull

and know before us
where danger lies,

so we must learn to go
soft-soled, tuned

to the jostle and churn
of unseen waters,

ankle-deep
in dew-drenched grass,

early morning meadows.

OF BIRDS AND BONES

FLOTILLA
'Heaven Scent' Magnolia

They tack in, full rig, under cover of darkness,
dock before dawn in cement-paved ports

at wharves of picket fence. The voyage
has been long through winter's bald estates,

gusting grit and dust have shred their sails
to votive rags, bound now to every leafless branch.

Waxen petals blood-tinged white
glow like manna at first light.

THE WATCH

At this moment in a park
in Paris, Lisbon or Shanghai,
men and women

dressed in black and grey and brown
gather into their heads,
lean into a game of chess,

their boards balanced
across makeshift tables
made from metal chairs.

With the concentration
of Cézanne's card players
they'll do the best they can:

bend over our destiny,
play against the clock.
Sane focus of a world

that runs rings around them
on sand and cinder tracks;
all-weather vigilantes

reading tea leaves
under the cast-iron awning
where they meet each afternoon.

SAN JUAN DE DIOS, GRANADA

I am washing dishes, my hands
plunged in lukewarm suds,
between sponge and plate
an image: that paupers' hospital
last seen twenty years ago,
the heat, the flaking plaster,
shuffling men in thin pyjamas,
felt slippers in the sun,
liver-spotted spectres
in and out of shade.

Another day, a village café
in the Pyrenees. It's Wednesday.
First drops of rain lead pellets
on the chestnut's palmate leaves,
pockmarks in the pink-brown dust,
our bare legs splattered
and the owner's tow-haired grandsons
balancing our plates across the yard
in slow procession.

But mostly it's a scene
I cannot place: a bend in the road,
the shade of fig trees,
a low wall mounted
with a stiff wire grille
and we are driving past –
the sort of moment, banal
and everyday, when nothing much
is going on, when you see there is
no turning back, just the on and on
around another bend for no reason.

GLASS HOUSE

He laughs sometimes,
and sometimes not,
mostly sleeps
in the phone booth
he has made his own
on the corner
of this Paris street
that smells of piss
and rotten wine,
his life open
for the world to see
through tempered panes.

He reads us
back into ourselves,
his eyes on ours
challenge us
to conjugate
his beard and breasts,
the brown bikini top.
As morning breaks
and pigeons roo-coo-coo,
he leaves his box,
relieves himself
and stands, his back
against a stout plane tree.

THE COPING STONE

It's not a weeping rock the faithful come to kneel at,
a stoup that never dries in the wall of a ruined church.

This slab is more enigma, a mystery dressed by hand
who knows how long ago. It lies inert – a fallen cap-

or coping stone – too thick to lift or shift. But, like you,
sometimes it happens: water wells, heaves up in lumps

from a source so deep memory cannot tell of it; tears
swell through weighted lids, untold grief tips over.

A Thousand Bars

I always thought Rilke's panther was black
until I learned of Ota Benga and went to see
the big cats still held in the Paris zoo.

The year they put Ota Benga behind bars in the Bronx
they made a bust of him in pure white plaster,
though he was black as I thought Rilke's panther

must have been. They labelled his bust 'Pygmy',
although Benga had a name and was, by then,
quite famous. He shared the cage with an orangutan,

Duhong, and a parrot whose name does not survive.
His teeth were filed to sharpened points,
a custom of his people, the Mbuti, to whom he once

belonged. When he bared them the crowd took it
for a grin. He was released before the year was out
(objections to man and monkey side by side).

A reverend paid to have his teeth crowned, put him
in a suit and took him to live in Lynchburg where
he was not lynched but never managed to escape

the *thousand bars* that stacked up wave on wave
between him and his lost world.
He paced the shrinking cage, his heart grew small.

When he knew there was to be no going home
he built a fire, chipped his teeth, stole a pistol,
shot himself and died. It was 1916. He was 32.

BASSO CONTINUO
for Vedran Smailović

It begins with a summer concert, wine. Red wine
carmine on white linen, evening light. Schubert's
Quintet in C. One cellist knows the score by heart,
turns his head, sees concentric rings

pulse in every glass. That night he dreams: a field,
bright air, the absent smell of death. No flies,
no sign the earth has been disturbed. He knows,
yet does not know he knows, what lies below or why.

No movement but his bow, his elbow back and forth.
Hoarse words hauled up, grim adagio.
He sows a solemn beauty and moves on:
another field, another town, another country.

Around our only world and round again, concentric
rings lapping the shores of every human heart.

FULL TILT

Sometimes you see a picture of a place
a long way off, a place you'll never go to,
not even with the longest life
or in your wildest dreams, with a name
you've never heard of, in a country
you have to look up on a map. A place where,
if you went, you wouldn't understand
a word the people said. Or what
the rules were.

           The ground shifts –
you put a hand out, your head
begins to turn, as though the earth
had started to spin faster
then faster, faster still.

Because that picture made you think
of other places, and then more places,
of small villages not unlike your own,
millions of them,
and you know each village lives
in its own world, just as yours does,
believing it is safe and everlasting. It's what

Copernicus must have felt
when he realised the earth
could not possibly be the apple
of God's eye. He must have pushed
the thought away, pretended
that he hadn't had it, until he could no longer
keep the knowledge out. For weeks,
for months, perhaps, his head so light,
his legs unsteady, his body nauseous
with all that motion, the disappearing sun.

PAX

A clutch of huts braced for dawn. Shadows sift
behind closed lids: sleep-staggered parents,
grandparents sick of someone else's war.

Another day.

Any minute now the skim of skyfire, roar
and smoke. Children struggle out of dreams,
out of the streams of dilute blood, cleft flesh

of melons crushed. Under the blasted baobab
a scratch of curs, nostrils flared to catch
the air's first stirring, ears alert.

They wait

and wait, muzzles nestled between paws, their eyes
uneasy under crumpled brows. Stars dull,
the far hill's lemon rim spreads up and out.

The village waits, wastes the first of daylight's hours.

INDIAN SUMMER

Sheer air lifts late flowers,
turns petals inside out, bends
stalks like pliant metal,
silvers grass.

Above, too high to cause alarm,
black specks drift on blue,
raptors wheeling.
The perfect autumn day.

And yet my body
missed a beat,
a sudden falling,
like floorboards giving
underneath my weight.

THE RED PLANE

Did we see it first, or hear
the high-pitched drone,
intermittent as a lawnmower?

A small red airplane,
swirling vapours
opening and closing

as it cartwheeled, looped
the loop, flaunted
its wild paces,

left us without the means
of measuring, no place still enough
to take our bearings, judge the scale.

Hair whipped our faces
as we threaded rocking cars,
fear wrapped us in its silence –

the flight ahead,
our lives entrusted
to a flailing metal case.

RAID

You cannot tell how fear
will cleave your body
until your turn comes.
They say a hare screams
louder than a hungry baby

but no scream reached me
that still November morning
as I watched from my window,
attracted by movement on the hill:
twelve men, long shadows

scattered in a dance or game,
an ancient form of chess
or hunt the *cailleach*.
They stalked the rushy slope,
high-stepped in and up,

tighter and closer,
until they were over the brow,
grouped behind a far stone wall.
I imagined the low tones, bare talk,
thought it was all done

until they appeared again, the hunt
not over yet, figures walking
the old green road, stooped
with the weight of poles and nets,
crates.

I looked back to the headland,
scanned the clumps of bent,
the short-cropped grass,
the hillside
desolate in the slanting light.

HOLY RUMBLE

The moon etches a limb of promise, a scratch,
a hairline crack through which the mind
may slither if it dares.

How strong our trust in absence is. We see
a picture of a cheese and smell it; smell
the lingering reek of goat and conjure up
those creatures of the hills, the way they stare.

Early morning, neither sound nor silence –
an agitation of ingredients, cosmic spin.
Poor, bare, forked animals, our blunt tines
cobbled tuning forks to probe the damp air,

fashion fairy tales from shadows, whistle
a happy tune. Like the holy rumble I read about,
a human prayer wheel powered by cloistered nuns
whose only task was keeping up their sacred hum,

leaving scientists to do the plumbing, tinker
with infinity, toss quarks and quasars
through doughnut holes, compute vast multiples
of trillions with an ease that leaves our politicians

flummoxed – while we turn silver
in our pockets, rumble on,
take comfort in the fact our earth is shared
by seven billion other human souls.

SMALL MERCY

Enfolded in an empty house,
    for living company a spider
    and a wilting basil plant,
rimmed round by stone

rolled back
    to the thick centre
    of silence
where the sun sings

to a crumb of bread
    and the spider's missing leg
    becomes the focus
of the morning's distillation.

Last night they jostled
    at the foot of the bed,
    the unnamed dead,
asked for nothing

save to be kept
    in our minds
    where the air is,
where we are.

Left meekly
    as obedient dogs,
    the last chill of camphor
breathed back into

the river-rounded stones
    of this penitential tholos:
    updraught of air, fresh earth,
the sweet breath of children.

DEIRBHILE

She was the amethyst sky before the dawn,
a hidden rustling in the grass;
she was the speckled eggs in the fuchsia hedge,
fragile, complete and full of longing.

She is her mother's soul's desire, its fire,
a steady flame with heart of snow.
She is running mountain water –
a daughter.

THE SYMMETRY OF DOMES

We sit cross-legged
in the deep-piled stillness
of an empty mosque,

thoughts loosen,
rise unhurried
as a lift of lapwings;

words drift
round and round,
our minds complete

each sphere, find comfort
in the wide-mouthed cups,
their ancient gloss.

OTHERWISE, STILLNESS
Heinrich Böll Cottage, Achill

The picture in the window does not move,
except for a caravan of snails
inching the horizon, except
where the sea's surface crawls.
You can make out its curled lip,
the slow snarl onto the beach.

Except for my eyes
probing the bushes
for robin, for wren.
Otherwise, stillness.

It is a painting, I another,
the two of us propped
against the walls of a corridor,
watching each other,
contemplating the width of our universe.

THE ROPE BRIDGE DREAM

All winter sewing shapes,
sorting, stitching,
standing back to look.

In the moon's blue chill
their brilliance fades,
reds turn to black,

green to grey,
fabrics fray
and spill.

A journey through the night,
an unmapped valley,
the promise of a bridge

that spans a deep ravine.
Boulders
cast silhouettes;

creatures rustle,
snakes;
an owl wings silently ahead.

Old rope, some weathered boards –
it barely holds:
a slip of string

dropped by a careless bird,
a chalk mark
scrawled across a glinting slate,

spun filament not fit to carry weight.

MAN ON WIRE, AUGUST 1974

Every time I see magpies
on a phone wire, tails
stiff rudders to the wind,
I think of Philippe Petit and his obsession
with tightrope walking.

Where do you go with your life
once you have fulfilled a dream,
exhausted the outermost reaches
of your passion
as he did

when he dallied forty-five minutes
four hundred metres in the air,
flirted with death
on a taut steel wire
strung between twin towers?

At first his face wore the maniacal mask
of concentration, his soft-soled slippers
symbiotic with the cable, a light breeze,
gulls below, and his long curved pole.
Once above the void

how the rictus seemed to melt
– almost a smile –
not for his friends, not for the police,
but because he knew that he had reached
his destination, the place all of his life had led to.

When magpies are thrown
into an irretrievable wobble
they fly to the shelter of trees.

I watch a man tease gravity,
lie down full length or kneel

on the thinnest of threads – how this fills me
with dread, scuppers the illusion
that I will always have something
to hold on to: an airplane's table and seat,
wheels tucked up beneath me, like feet.

FLENSED

She hung from the ledge
   of their marriage,
         ropes chafed her skin.

Ignorant of anatomy, unprepared
   for blood, her tongue was a tool
         she had not learned to hone.

His was steel. It leafed
   through muscle, eeled
         its tempered tip round

startled bone, revealed
   a glint of opal,
         articulation's nub.

Ariadne in Villecroze

It makes sense to stand at the corner
of the village square gorging pigeons
on stale bread, pelting women
with profanities or hurling curses at cars
driven by young men.

Perfect sense to stand there
dressed in mauve, the way you were
that day fifty years ago
when he sailed off, your life aborted
in a cloud of diesel fumes and dust.

To rage and spit your bile
on half a century of loss.

MEMENTO

With the tip of a small kitchen knife
she makes the first incision, prises
the cap, lifts the round crown,
a penny for her thoughts;

with a surgeon's precision,
as if her life hung on it, she cuts
five deep slits, makes a pithy map
for parting, takes care to stop short

of the taut sacs of sap,
sealed and dry as human skin
and just as thin. She eases each flap,
one eye on where he lies.

Flesh parts from flesh
in slow disunion. An oily spray
betrays her – she leaves
the orange lotus by his pillow.

DISCLAIMER

La mer n'est pas une flaque d'eau
– *Libération* headline, 29 July 2013

The mountain did not mean to be so high,
the water did not want to run so fast
down rocky beds of stone and grit.

The grassy slopes that catch the rain-filled
clouds are sorry that they made you slip
and gave the sheep sore feet. Along the shore

the sand's intention was not to clog
the cogwheels of the engine, or your teeth.
The sea would rather be all surface, not so deep.

DEALING WITH BEARS

The former US bomber pilot
    (who runs a B&B
        in Scotland now)

told me over breakfast
    and his wife's good jam
        about bears –

how as a boy he played
    at hunting them
        but not for real

stalking the fields
    around his grandma's house
        with a homemade bow.

She always had a stick
    to beat the saucepan with
        when she took him

picking blackberries
    to scare them bears away.
        He also told me

what to do
    if ever I came head-to-
        head with one:

stand your ground, he said,
    if he comes for you
        lie face down,

you may get mauled a bit
    but you won't get killed. And
        never look 'em in the eye.

So I don't.
     Not in my neighbour's
         daft dog's eyes

as she tangles slipknots
     round my ankles; not
         in the bullock's

tetchy with testosterone
     when he blocks my path
         to home. And nor do you

who tell me you will not
     stare down the pin-eyed crab
         the doctors say is there

not yet
     not until
         not unless

it sidles out of its concealment
     pincers raised
         spoiling for a fight.

LE JARDINIER VALLIER
after Cézanne

There is an ease slips through the body
after work well done. The heart
minds its own business, leaves alone
the slack repose of limb and bone.

On summer days we'd find him there,
still as a lizard by the orchard wall,
hat over his eyes, his hands asleep
on his thighs. The chair
was never moved. *C'est la chaise
de Monsieur Vallier*, we were told.

As if this explained everything –
the silence of his deer-like tread,
his loping gait. The way he came
and went unseen. How the garden
sang with light and shade.

AIDE-MÉMOIRE

For me love is the true colour, the true matter of art
– Marc Chagall

On days when I write
in palest grey
or black
or white so faint I cannot see

I think of Chagall
a volcano of fireworks
          exploding
around him

a kaleidoscope
               of diced suns

more than canvas could hold

until he reached for ceilings
would have painted the sky
had he found ladder long enough.

He turned to windows
the glory of stained glass

radiant partitions

between his heart
and the world.

VAGRANT

The quiet in the church
has the quality of slate,
that smooth sliding.
This is where
she sheltered as a girl,
listened while

the soft-faced priest
preached
from the sculpted pulpit
about baking,
the jar of flour,
how, if you tap it gently,

there's always room
for a little more; about the wheatear,
its flash of hope.
Today the incense
is residual,
a faint stain

on the hanging air. She hears
nothing, barely
her own blood,
the far-off cries
of children.
Alone

in a place not her own
without invitation, without
trespass. A sanctuary still.

HIDE

The layers build up,
skin on skin,
as grief accretes
like paint.

The gloss of years
may seem
distressed
but like old leather

it has weathered,
an old skiff
out at sea,
its barnacled hull

a medalled chest,
hard-won armour,
watertight, shipshape,
almost free.

TRESPASS

A figure watches from the looking glass
as I cross the landing at first light.

Outside young crows squabble;
willows wave new growth; a lamb
calls for its mother. I see mine.

Shadows furrow her naked face,
a woman startled by intruding age.

Between London and York

I see my reflection
in the steady stare
of the child
across the aisle

and I am not *a woman startled*
by intruding age, but old,
the far side of the river,
bags around my feet.

OF BIRDS AND BONES

My bones are threaded
with the snicker of gulls,
feathers of the old familiar,
lost conversations, ghosts.

I read about it long ago,
how bones record and store
as tree rings do – the years
of drought, the storms.

Stories rise
on a drift of marrow
and last night the old place,
illumined in the dark,
fell open
like a house of cards.

But I am here.

Starlings tut-tut
as I walk my teeming body
towards the sun
still rising in the east.

The years have brought
new gifts: grumbling fulmars
perched on ledges,
a flat sea ironed to a crease.

And from below
the crumbling cliff
burbled woodnotes,
unearthly music,
eider courting.

The Forbearance of Trees

Grass runs silver-backed
across the empty meadow
where a woman stands
and from behind a low stone wall
observes the glow that fills each porthole
of this house that has not sailed,
or sunk, in forty years.

Anchored in the swell of dawn
it rides the silence. She watches
through a net of winter trees,
their patient arms.

TYPEWRITTEN

A sequence in the thrush's evening repertoire
– a rattle of staccato among the juicy riffs –
and in the time it takes the clicks and ticks
to come around again your message hoofs its way
across a page, divots fly, the metal keys
colts' feet, the ribbon beaten to within an inch
of its already faded life, now black, now blank.

How we all beat out our longings in those days
like linen on a rock, embraced the distance metal
brought, pounded the molten alphabet as if by force
alone we could gain access to an alien heart. Or,
lovesick, typed languidly, morosely tipped each key,
then pressed the sleek steel lever; heard the cogs en-
gage, the ratchet flay emotion down the dented page.

ÉVASION

We set out at cross purposes,
his *sensible* sparring with my sensitive;
his proposal of a *promenade* when I wanted
a lonely country walk.

As if our eyes said one thing
and our lips another
yet words were all we
listened out for,

ears sharp as scissors
to trim the letters
to shapes we knew,
familiar landmarks

on a foreign road.
Two blind beggars
we stumbled on,
struck shins and elbows

against glottal plosives,
rough-cut consonants,
stubbed our toes
on *double entendres*

until I accused him
of evasion and he said yes!
locked his eyes on mine, yes!
he said, and grabbed my hand.

WALTZ

I was driving home all eyes,
pupils splashed to saturation
by the spill of August rain,

when a shaft of music
roused my dozing eardrums –
an old familiar waltz and it was

France again, a village schoolhouse,
an impromptu tea dance
in an upstairs sitting room.

Crystal jugs and goblets in glass cases
jostle softly as couples laugh their feet
through foxtrot, tango … waltz.

I never knew his name,
can no longer see his face –
somebody's young husband,

as I was a young wife. My body
holds the memory: sweet fusion,
brief encounter, two errant souls.

IS THIS WHERE LOVE LURKS
Aesculus x carnea

A honeyed tree with dark pink flowers,
yellow throats. Incandescence.
Bursts of fire.

Is that the key, a clue
to why I've fallen
for this spindly chestnut tree?

As trees go it's a child,
Degas' *Little Dancer*,
kid sister to the tall dudes down the yard,

their tar-stained candles stubbed
in shocks of fresh-washed green.
My tree's leaves are darker, slighter,

its blooms still blaze. Soon
these petals too will fall,
leaves begin to rust –

but that won't stop her dancing,
skirts skirling, skinny knees.

WARNING SHOTS

When you live on the edge
of an ocean, you cannot pretend
you did not see it coming.

The leaves are still, birds
chatter, the sea is a sheet
of steel. But out west

where last night the sun
left a sky illumined
like stained glass

dirt heaps up,
someone else's dustpan
emptied on your doorstep

and a magpie
rattling gunfire
at first light.

NIGHT VISITOR

All January an animal
on the windowsill at night,
some big cat too dark to see
crouched between window
and railings, in the space
made for flowers.

We wake to its growl,
a scratch on the glass, the lash
of its tail on the pane.
Some nights it howls
hour on hour, some nights
its eyes sprinkle stars.

In the morning the place
empty, darker than before,
hairs snagged in the ironwork,
whiffs of zoo. When we try to get
closer, a purring, a wheedling,
pleading to get in.

LURCH

What if the world did shift
on its axis, made bockety turns,
sent hiccups through
day after day?

The view from our window
has already moved. The landscape
has split, slipped like the hill
above Leenane, or ice.

Ripped. Then silence.
No sound returning
of bird, or you calling.

CLOSEDOWN

When I stood beside you
and you said nothing,
how could I guess

the inside of your head
was the colour of copper,
a dull sheen

slipping the curved walls
and the cavity empty
as a banquet hall

after a wedding,
the guests gone back
along grass-choked lanes,

not so much as the echo
of a song, the skitter of mice
on the crumb-strewn floor.

How could you tell me your fear,
as you pointed to the plum glow
on the window frame,

that words can disappear,
a whole vocabulary,
the skull's vaulted recess

a flickering screen.

HANDLE WITH CARE

I

You wake to your heart
pacing bare boards
in an upstairs room,
your face strewn
with questions.

First dawn back in the city
and it has not stopped –
the hum of rope
round and round
above the fretful streets.

Stoppered bottles
pack the shelves
inside your head.
Your mouth smiles
but your eyes do not look out.

II

The air taut
with unspilled rain
and you,
inside the house,
an unsprung coil.

Ease the wire,
let loose the string,
turn the peg
before the catgut snaps,
before the cable

slips its cleat, stings you
with its bloody whip,
before glass shatters
                    drifts
round your bare feet.

Be the hawser's wormcast
on a summer foredeck,
soak up
late evening's oily sun.

GEMINIDS

It was Jupiter slung sharp and steady
from the tip of a gelid moon
that had us out there
scoured by frost
at the edge of the concrete yard,

scanning the open dome, the roof
that lets through snow and wind, mystery
and fear, the upper limit
of our understanding beyond which
words fail, fall like spent stars.

And fall they did. Not stars but blazing dust motes,
the first as fleeting as a skim of headlights
glimpsed behind a hill, brief
exhalations, magnesium flares
from the floating tin can man.

As our eyes filled up with dark, matching
their contours to the curve of sky, hidden hands
lobbed missiles from all sides, crystals
caught in lucent flight, coating next morning's garden
with fine powder, like spent thought.

DISARMED

Words are the part of silence that can be spoken
– Jeanette Winterson

I lie in the dark, picture
the garden filling with birds,
stencil shapes
perched in the fretwork
of leafless trees: chaffinch, robin,
goldcrest, sparrow, tit.

I search for words
to clothe my thoughts in, flounder
in a pile of dislocated syllables.
I trawl and trawl but bring up only
pebbles, a gritty residue of silt.

p. 18: 'A Thousand Bars': In 1906, at almost exactly the time Rilke wrote 'The Panther', which appeared in his *New Poems* (1907), the following notice appeared on the bars of a cage at the zoo in the Bronx, New York:

> *The African Pigmy, "Ota Benga."*
> *Age, 23 years. Height, 4 feet 11 inches.*
> *Weight, 103 pounds. Brought from the*
> *Kasai River, Congo Free State, South Cen-*
> *tral Africa, by Dr. Samuel P. Verner. Ex-*
> *hibited each afternoon during September*

Ota Benga's bust was on display in an exhibition, 'The Invention of the Savage', at the anthropological museum, Musée du Quai Branly, Paris in 2012.

p. 19: 'Basso Continuo': In May 1992, Vedran Smailović, aka The Cellist of Sarajevo, played Albinoni's Adagio in G minor on the site of the bomb that killed 22 people queuing for bread in Sarajevo. He repeated this gesture at sites of atrocities and disasters around the world.

p. 24: 'Raid': *Cailleach*: the Irish for old woman or hag. In folklore, the hare was often thought to be an old woman in disguise.

p. 49: 'Évasion': In French, *sensible* = sensitive; *promenade* = a walk; *évasion* = escape (as well as evasion).

ACKNOWLEDGEMENTS

Acknowledgements are due to the editors of the following publications where some of the poems, or versions of them, first appeared: *Abridged, New Hibernia Review, Poetry Ireland Review, The Clifden Anthology, Cyphers, The Poddle, The Rialto, The Stinging Fly, Crannóg, Sligo Poets' Calendar 2014, Southword, Stony Thursday, The SHOp*.

'Basso Continuo' won the 2012 Trócaire-Poetry Ireland poetry competition. It has appeared in Bosnian in *Oslobođenje*, Sarajevo.

'Flotilla', through *Abridged* and The Verbal Arts Centre, Derry, was chosen for outdoor display at the Southbank Centre's Festival of Britain 60th anniversary celebrations in London in 2011.

'Flensed' was shortlisted for the Poetry on the Lake competition 2013.

'Typewritten' came third in the 2010 Dromineer Literary Festival poetry competition.

The author is grateful to An Chomhairle Ealaíon/The Arts Council for a Literature Bursary which made the completion of this collection possible.

Special thanks to Alan Hayes of Arlen House and to my writerly friends for their sharp eyes and ears.

ABOUT THE AUTHOR

Geraldine Mitchell's first collection, *World Without Maps*, was published by Arlen House in 2011. She lives near Louisburgh, Co. Mayo. Previous publications include two novels for young people and a biography. Geraldine won the Patrick Kavanagh Poetry Award in 2008.